I0814280

EXTREME SPORTS EVENTS

DAKAR RALLY

LUKE HANLON

SportsZone

An Imprint of Abdo Publishing

abdobooks.com

abdobooks.com

Published by Abdo Publishing, a division of ABDO, PO Box 398166, Minneapolis, Minnesota 55439.

Printed in the United States of America, North Mankato, Minnesota.
102023
012024

Cover Photo: Franck Fife/AFP/Getty Images
Interior Photos: Franck Fife/AFP/Getty Images, 4–5, 6, 16–17, 18, 20–21, 23, 26, 27, 29; Red Line Editorial, 9; Dean Mouhtaropoulos/Getty Images Sport/Getty Images, 10–11, 13; Marcelo Maragni/Red Bull Content/AP Images, 14; Victor R. Caivano/AP Images, 24–25

Editors: Charlie Beattie and Steph Giedd
Series Designer: Cynthia Della-Rovere

Library of Congress Control Number: 2023939469

Publisher's Cataloging-in-Publication Data

Names: Hanlon, Luke, author.
Title: Dakar Rally / by Luke Hanlon
Description: Minneapolis, Minnesota: Abdo Publishing, 2024 | Series: Extreme sports events | Includes online resources and index.
Identifiers: ISBN 9781098292348 (lib. bdg.) | ISBN 9798384910282 (ebook)
Subjects: LCSH: Extreme sports--Juvenile literature. | Action sports (Extreme sports) --Juvenile literature. | Off-road racing--Juvenile literature. | Motor vehicle sports--Juvenile literature. | Dune buggy racing--Juvenile literature.
Classification: DDC 796.046--dc23

TABLE OF CONTENTS

CHAPTER 1

CRASHING OUT

The Dakar Rally is considered the most grueling motorsport race in the world. Not many people know more about the challenges of the Dakar than Carlos Sainz Sr. The native of Spain began driving in the Dakar in 2006. He went on to win the rally in 2010, 2018, and 2020. In 2023 he was still competing at the age of 60.

Sainz was able to make it through the first five days of competition in 2023 driving for Team Audi Sport. But even the most experienced drivers can face trouble when dealing with the challenges of the Dakar. On the sixth day of the rally, Sainz's teammate and 14-time champion Stéphane Peterhansel crashed his car. Sainz was closely following Peterhansel, which caused him to crash as well.

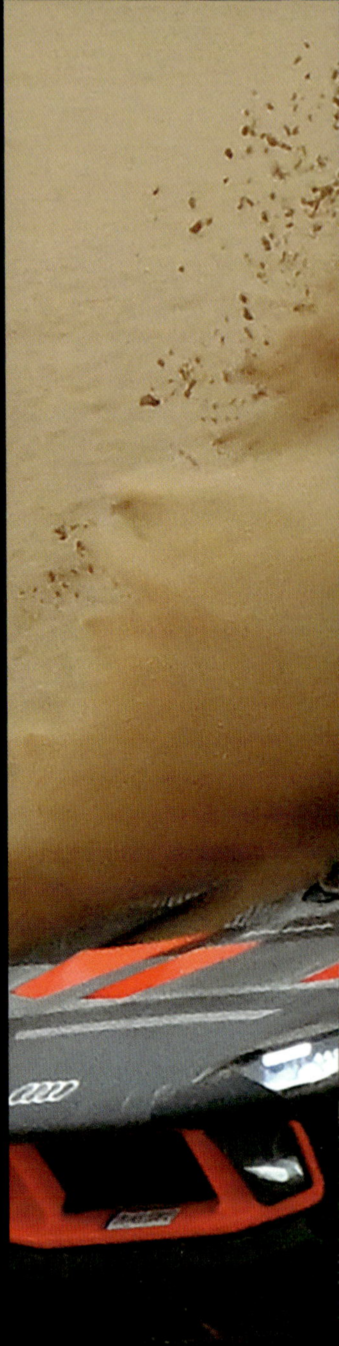

Carlos Sainz Sr. competed for Team Audi Sport in the 2023 Dakar Rally.

Sainz is assessed for injuries after his crash during the 2023 Dakar Rally.

Peterhansel withdrew from the race. Due to the time lost, Sainz had no chance of winning a fourth title. But he continued to race.

Four days later, Sainz faced more problems. He drove aggressively off the top of a sand dune. The front of his car dove straight into the sand, causing the vehicle to flip over. Sainz and his navigator, Lucas Cruz, were able to get out of the car and right it again. However, Sainz was also experiencing a lot of chest pain.

A medical helicopter came to get Sainz and take him to a local hospital. However, going to the hospital would have meant being disqualified from the race. Sainz told the pilot to bring him back to his car. He only withdrew after realizing his car was too wrecked to repair.

While Sainz thought he had avoided serious injury, he later went to the hospital with back pain. He had broken his back in two places in the area between his shoulder blades. The challenges of the Dakar Rally can be too much to overcome, even for the toughest and most experienced drivers.

LOST IN THE DESERT

The Dakar Rally was created because of a mistake. In 1977 Thierry Sabine got lost in the Libyan desert while competing on his motorbike in the Abidjan-Nice Rally. He was fascinated by the challenges of the landscape. Over the course of the three days he was lost, Sabine came up with the idea of the Dakar Rally, a race that would start in Paris, France, and end in Dakar, Senegal. He worked to organize the race once he returned to France. The first Dakar Rally was ready to start by December 26, 1978. The route ran through six countries and spanned 6,200 miles (10,000 km). Cars, motorcycles, and trucks all competed in the first event. In 1980 the race was divided into different classes for the three types of vehicles.

The route of the race changes each year. But for the first 12 years of the rally, every route started in Paris and ended in Dakar. That lasted until 1992. That year's race still started in Paris, but it ended in Cape Town, South Africa. Then in 1995, the race started in Grenada, Spain, instead of Paris. As the starting and ending points continued to change throughout the years, the rally ran through different parts of Europe and Africa. The structure of the Dakar was changed forever in 2008 when four French citizens were murdered in the African country of Mauritania, which was one of the countries on that year's route. There were also terrorist threats made against the event. Fearing drivers would not be safe racing through the region, organizers canceled the event. Starting in 2009, the rally was moved to South America. Until 2019, drivers raced through different South American countries. Argentina, Chile, and Peru were the countries used most often for the Dakar. Then, in 2020, the organizers of the rally decided to move the race to run only in Saudi Arabia. The Middle Eastern country has more than one million square miles

1979 DAKAR RALLY ROUTE

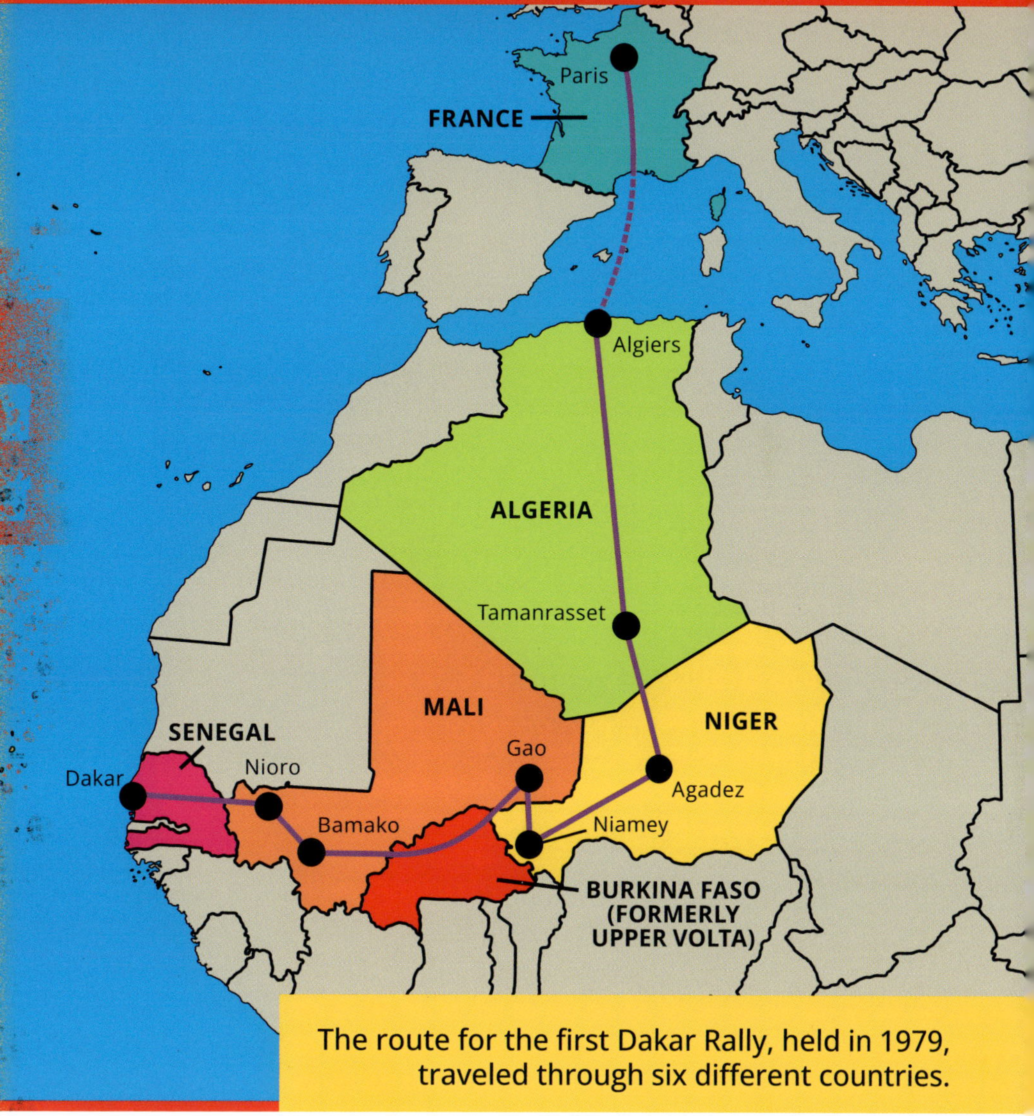

The route for the first Dakar Rally, held in 1979, traveled through six different countries.

(2.6 million sq km) of desert, and its hot temperatures keep with the spirit of the original race philosophy.

CHAPTER 2

TO THE LIMIT

Drivers must prepare themselves physically and mentally for the two-week challenge of the Dakar Rally. Competitors must be ready to handle continuous hours of driving in scorching heat where anything can go wrong at any moment. The rugged terrain also needs to be considered while training.

To get into physical shape, drivers will work out for months before the race. Dakar motorcycle champion Cyril Despres has a workout routine on the official Dakar website for other motorcyclists to use. It focuses on building riders' core and arm muscles. That can help them stay balanced while riding on the shifting desert sand.

Cyril Despres won the Dakar Rally's motorcycle category five times.

Being in good physical shape also helps competitors deal with the extreme weather in the desert. During the day, temperatures there can reach up to 122 degrees Fahrenheit (50°C). To get themselves used to these conditions, drivers do cardio workouts in incredibly hot conditions. Leading up to the 2016 Dakar, driver Harry Hunt rode on a stationary bike for 50 minutes at a time in a room that was 95 degrees Fahrenheit (35°C). This prepared his body for the heat. It also got his mind ready for the stress that hot conditions can create.

Knowing how to stay hydrated during the rally is another important part of training. Drivers must wear full body gear to protect themselves from possible fires if they crash. Those extra layers cause the drivers to sweat a lot each day. During training, drivers keep track of how much water they've lost through sweat. If drivers know before the race how much they need to drink, that can help them avoid dehydration when it matters most. They also are

ALTITUDE TRAINING

Another way drivers get used to the environment of the rally is by training in locations with high altitude. Some Dakar courses have reached elevations of 15,100 feet (4,600 m) or even higher.

The Dakar Rally can be incredibly dangerous. Riders wear protective equipment to prevent injuries such as broken bones and burns.

Members of the Red Bull KTM Factory Racing team celebrate at the finish line in 2023.

careful to add supplements to their water to replace lost electrolytes and salt.

Drivers go to these lengths to simulate the route's conditions for a reason. They are not allowed to train on the route itself. If drivers are caught on the route before the race begins, they can be suspended from competing in the race for up to two years.

QUALIFYING FOR DAKAR

Anyone who is 18 or older can enter the Dakar if they have a driver's license from the Fédération Internationale de l'Automobile (FIA), the governing body of auto racing. This opens the opportunity to not only professional drivers who are supported by a team, but also amateur racers who want to test their skills. The only other requirement for amateurs to qualify for the Dakar is that they must complete one FIA-recognized rally before the Dakar. This is a good way for drivers to prepare themselves for the challenges of the race. It also lets the FIA know that the amateurs are serious about competing in such an intimidating event.

To encourage more amateurs to participate in the rally, its organizers started a racing series called the Road to Dakar. The series is a set of five races held in different countries around the world. And these races serve as more than just the best form of training for the Dakar. There is a prize for each race as well. The winners of each race get free entry into the upcoming Dakar Rally. Depending on the type of vehicle they compete in, that can save drivers tens of thousands of dollars.

CHAPTER 3

DEALING WITH THE DESERT

The Dakar is the world's most dangerous motorsport race for many reasons. The length of the rally is a main one. Over the 16 days of the 2023 rally, drivers traveled approximately 3,100 miles (5,000 km). The biggest challenge of traveling that far is the number of miles drivers have to cover in a single day. Every Dakar is broken up into stages, and each stage takes place over the course of a day. Each driver must complete every stage to stay in the race. Every day is different during the rally, but some stages cover as much as 500 miles (805 km). On average, a single stage of the Dakar is as long as the total length of many rally events in the world.

To keep weight down, the cargo spaces in Dakar trucks remain mostly empty during the race.

Huge sand dunes are just one of the challenges competitors face as they race across the desert.

If drivers had to cover this distance on a paved road the entire time, it wouldn't be much of a challenge. What makes the distance difficult is the route's terrain. Most of the course runs through desert, so vehicles must travel over sand dunes. Sand can create major issues for tires, causing vehicles to get stuck. The drivers reach speeds of up to 112 miles per hour (180 km/h), which puts added strain on the vehicles. And other portions of the route might involve driving over streams, gravel roads, and large rocks.

STRESS AND STRAIN

The hot temperatures, rough terrain, and continuous hours of driving cause a lot of mental stress for drivers. Losing focus for even a second can result in a dangerous crash. In 2006 actor Charley Boorman filmed a documentary of himself competing in the Dakar on a motorcycle. Five days into the race, he crashed his motorcycle and broke both of his hands.

Boorman was lucky he only had broken bones, though. Some crashes at the Dakar have been much worse, as there have been 76 reported deaths since the first year of the rally. In addition, race spectators have also been killed by crashes.

Once drivers reach the end of a stage, the difficulties are not over for the day. After they've dealt with scorching daytime temperatures, it can get quite cold in the desert at night. Temperatures can drop to as low as 23 degrees

Sometimes drivers can continue on with the race even after a crash.

Fahrenheit (−5°C). For professional drivers with entire teams and a basecamp, this isn't too tough to deal with. But amateur drivers might have only a tent to sleep in, making the cold harder to handle.

TRAGIC ENDING

After coming up with the idea for the Dakar Rally in 1977, Thierry Sabine lost his life during the 1986 race. However, he wasn't participating in that year's event. Sabine was in a helicopter searching for lost vehicles in the sand dunes of Mali in West Africa. A sandstorm caused the helicopter to crash, killing Sabine and four other people who were on board.

It's key for the drivers to begin the recovery process before the race has even ended. At the end of each stage, drivers eat, hydrate, and clean themselves up at their campsites. Some drivers even have massage therapists to help with muscle aches or cramps.

Amateur drivers have less time to rest, as they have to prepare their own food, repair their own vehicles, and map out the next day's route all by themselves. A lot of this work is done by the team that travels with a professional driver. And while the end of a stage can be relaxing for the professionals, it can be the most stressful part of the day for their teams. The moment a stage ends, navigators get to work by going over the challenges of the next stage's route. With hundreds of miles to account for, this can take hours. That gives the navigators little time to rest. Team mechanics also work overnight to fix any damage that the rough terrain has caused to a vehicle.

Many drivers have crews to make repairs at the end of each stage. However, sometimes drivers must make their own repairs midrace in order to keep going.

CHAPTER 4

ROAD TO RECOVERY

The Dakar Rally now has five different divisions that drivers can race in. Finishing in first place in any of the divisions earns the driver a cash prize. Any driver who finishes in the top five of a division receives cash as well. The amount of money won is different every year, and it varies in each division. In 2023 the prize for first place for Utility Terrain Vehicle (UTV) drivers was $25,000. All other vehicles were awarded $45,000 for a first-place finish. Drivers make more from their sponsorships, however. Sponsors offer bonuses to their drivers if they win the division. In 2023 those bonuses ranged from $300,000 to $450,000.

While there is a lot of money to be won, most drivers who compete in the Dakar are not

Many drivers in the car category choose to drive small cars.

A driver inspects his car after flipping over during the 2023 Dakar Rally.

focused on winning the race. Just finishing the Dakar is a massive achievement. When the race was first run in 1978, 182 vehicles entered, but only 74 of them made it to the finish line in Dakar. The longest route the race has ever seen was in 1986 at roughly 9,300 miles (15,000 km). That year only 100 of the 482 drivers were able to finish the race. One of the rally's event directors has noted, "If everybody finished the race, it wouldn't be the Dakar."

The drivers' emotions after they cross the finish line showcase how difficult it is to successfully make it through the rally. Some drivers can't hold back tears when they win the race, knowing how much effort they had to put in to do so. Other drivers seem to be more relieved that the race is over. A lot of them have dirt or mud all over their faces from that day's stage.

BACK FOR MORE

Even though the race takes a toll on a driver's body and mind, the feeling of finishing makes drivers want to come back. That's especially true for the winners. There are

Ricky Brabec powers his bike through the sand during the 2020 Dakar Rally.

dozens of drivers who have won the Dakar multiple times. It took Ricky Brabec five years of training and preparation before he became the first American to win the Dakar in 2020. When he was asked what he was planning to do after winning the race, he said, "We're going to try to do the exact same thing we did this year next year."

It can take up to a month for a driver's body to fully recover from finishing the Dakar. Recovery time can be even longer for drivers who have suffered injuries while they were competing. Despite the risks, drivers know it's worth the pain and stress to be able to finish something so incredible. It's why drivers from countries around the world flock to the race every year to compete in the toughest motorsport event on Earth.

BACK ON THE BIKE

During the Dakar in 2021, motorcyclist C. S. Santosh hit a rock and fell hard into a sand dune. He was put into a medically induced coma for eight days to help with healing. After eight months of recovery, Santosh was able to ride on a motorcycle again. That's when he began training to compete in a future edition of the Dakar. In 2023 he announced that he was aiming to make his return the following year.

Kevin Benavides of Argentina won the motorbike division of the Dakar Rally in 2023.

GLOSSARY

altitude
The height of a thing or point above sea level.

amateur
A person who competes in a sport without getting paid.

cardio
Exercise that elevates one's heart rate.

dehydration
A condition in which the body does not have enough water.

medically induced coma
A prolonged period of unconsciousness used to protect the brain after an illness or injury.

motorsport
A sport involving the racing of vehicles.

sand dune
A hill of sand that is formed by wind.

sponsorships
Money given to athletes in return for supporting a company's products publicly.

terrain
The physical qualities of the land within a region.

MORE INFORMATION

BOOKS

Hewson, Anthony K. *Auto Racing Strategies*. Minneapolis, MN: Abdo Publishing, 2024.

Hustad, Douglas. *Innovations in Auto Racing*. Minneapolis, MN: Abdo Publishing, 2022.

Rule, Heather. *GOATs of Auto Racing*. Minneapolis, MN: Abdo Publishing, 2022.

ONLINE RESOURCES

To learn more about the Dakar Rally, please visit **abdobooklinks.com** or scan this QR code. These links are routinely monitored and updated to provide the most current information available.

INDEX

ABOUT THE AUTHOR

Luke Hanlon is a sportswriter and editor based in Minneapolis.